P9-DTA-690

DiVida

Vida

MONICA A. HAND

Alice James Books
Farmington, Maine
www.alicejamesbooks.org

10 9 8 7 6 5 4 3 2 1

Alice James Books are published by Alice James Poetry Cooperative, Inc., an affiliate of the University of Maine at Farmington.

Alice James Books
114 Prescott Street
Farmington, ME 04938
www.alicejamesbooks.org

Library of Congress Cataloging-in-Publication Data

Names: Hand, Monica A., author.
Title: DiVida : poems / by Monica A. Hand.
Description: Farmington, ME : Alice James Books, [2018]
Identifiers: LCCN 2017052423 (print) | LCCN 2017055057 (ebook) | ISBN
    9781938584787 (eBook) | ISBN 9781938584749 (softcover : acid-free paper)
Classification: LCC PS3608.A69924 (ebook) | LCC PS3608.A69924 A6 2018 (print)
    | DDC 811/.6--dc23
LC record available at https://lccn.loc.gov/2017052423

Alice James Books gratefully acknowledges support from individual donors, private foundations, the University of Maine at Farmington, the National Endowment for the Arts, and the Amazon Literary Partnership.

ART WORKS. arts.gov

amazon *literary*
partnership

Cover art: "Butterflies," Krista Franklin, Collage on paper, 2013

Contents

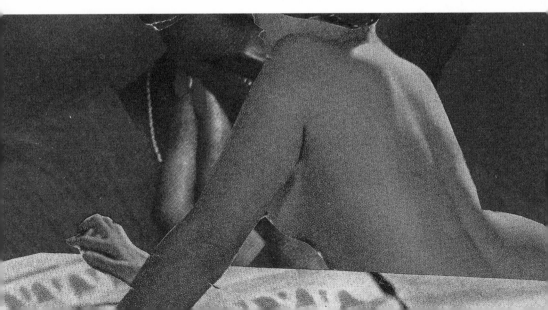

Acknowledgments

The poems listed here first appeared, sometimes in slightly different versions, in the following publications:

American Creative Writers on Class, ed. Oliver de la Paz, Rebecca Keith, Matthea Harvey, et al. (Big Wonderful Press, LLC, 2012): "DiVida lives within her means"

Drunken Boat: "DiVida guns the snow-white light," and "DiVida learns how to breathe."

Black Renaissance Noire: "In the end," "The Highway Patrol stop DiVida," "DiVida meets Trayvon Martin on the street and it is raining," "DiVida succumbs along the ridges of Brain Man," and "DiVida reads Brain Man's tarot at the Shady Oaks Trailer Park in Mosquito City."

Spoon River Poetry Review: "Postman."

The Lake Rises anthology: "DiVida dies," "DiVida stays awake until day breaks (remixed)," and "Stayed drunk."

The Mom Egg: "DiVida becomes pine"

Valley Voices: "DiVida posts black"

———

"…One is not oneself, one is several, incomplete, and subject to dispersal."

—Lyn Hejinian

"Multiple personas are how the African-American survives in society.
At the same time, donning these different masks could make them crazy
unless they learn how to syncopate them.

In every aspect of her life, at work, at home, with her lovers,
and in her dreams – she is a different person. She wants to be one person –
the same everywhere, one with everyone."

— from *The Book of DiVida*

———

DiVida I am's

after John Berryman

I am crooked petticoat jamboree
　　a tall girl whose balding bleeds
I am the magistrate's fool
　　so smart I do public school
I am a terrestrial body float
　　ocean the tsunami broke

I am the enemy of the sublime
　　slow move tractor slime
I am civil service blow
　　Wall Street man who hugs your dough
I am transformer queer in surplus drag
　　a woman whose tits sag

I am Afghan soldier with two hands dear
　　peace-keeping deaf eye blind ear
I am the homeless who wash in sinks
　　whose full-bodied veils chink
Decorated soldier in parade
　　the war on democracy terror raids

I am the off-key subway balladeer
    who cries *foul uncle* on TV
I am uptown bodega snow
    twin-tower afterglow
I am a Zipcar stalled in park
    leap year evangelist's bark

It's all clear at the family barbeque
    why grandpa spews tobacco
why kissing cousins snake and break
    why global greedy bastards gape
In vain   in vain   in vain it's all the same
    I am DiVida. My every name.

In the end

Electra demanded blood
Antigone longed for her undefiled body

I felt my own terribleness
as if the façade of God were all that I had left

God could not help this smelly
corpse   No god could meld

the fractured pieces of mythology
directed from stage left to stage right :::

revenge and rebirth in equal
distance from the center

of disarticulate thought

Masks for the madhouse

the singular, second-person and the third:: subjunctive, imperative
the same

the feminine
singular, neuter plural of

identify the object of
you name me

I am speaking to you
you have I have

into the workplace, marketplace, home place, the lover, the city, the zoo,
the nursery, jail, foreign, familiar, empty, scary, small overcrowded places

you give me no choice
my choice no choice

visible scar like the blackened eye
bruised arm like the wet bed
wet mop like the very wet panties
deafening quiet like a secondhand hum

a body that builds upon itself
                 masks the madhouse

it is easy to confuse what is with what is real
common names and proper ones the same

Othello at a house party

is afraid
to leave the safety

of the basement
armchair

put his purse unattended
on the floor

he loves to dance
but does not

voices in his head
call him unworthy

plague him
with questions:

is that blood on your hands
is it witchcraft that lures

Desdemona to hover
near you

to laugh at your jokes
she doesn't care

about your exploits or ambition
she is a gold-digging whore

how much money
do you even have Moor

just wait she will cuckold you
once she sees how black

you really are

Mythology

These were the years when the earth weighted towards falling:

the years of the black president

when the middle-class slept in their cars and their pure-blood children
knew songs of want, like the poor.

War ravaged every continent and our overfed and undernourished
   bodies.

This place called Manhattan (cluster that once held slaves)
boasted diminished belief in oppression.

It was a lie.

The God of many names: Jehovah, Allah, Buddha, Money – could not
   save us.

At the dawn of these times, Aaron begat nine daughters and a son;
demons seduced the boy and he died before he could make progeny.

But, the girls had plenty — bastard children of bad men.

Now, only one daughter remains and she sleeps rage and spews vile.

Mythology

No happy-ending story,
just the same ol' story.

Her mother, the first of the sisters to marry
in a wedding like a Grimm fairy story,

starring Sidney Poitier and Dorothy Dandridge;
he a Korean War hero in this story.

Dead rose bush and a stranded console TV,
snuffed by a cigarette left lit, became her story.

No more home in the suburbs and chickens,
sins of the father come home to roost.

The brutal father, the wasted father
the absent father, same ol' tired story

retold like in a Greek play
with masked prophecy and a neglectful, spiteful god.

DiVida splits her heirs

Zip your mouth darkie, Thomas Jefferson says in her dream.
DiVida shakes nasty.
Her bloodline clots.

Man is the only animal which devours his own kind,
is written on his and her tombstones.
She tries to wake with fits and starts

like a bad carburetor.
Her cousin is on the telephone,
wants her to sign the petition,

claim she is a descendent and dependent
on the Monticello clan,
wants her to dream in *Step and Fetch It*.

But she is insufficient evidence.
Sally H is talking inside her head: *He was not a perfect man*.
Everybody knows he would not fuck a child.

Men do not fuck children.
Masters do not fuck their slaves.
He was the pinnacle of these United States.

What other lie is there to tell?
I wasn't his mistress.
I was his wife.

DiVida wakes at the cemetery
where the family hold white lilies
and eat dandelion greens.

Discourse on how Sapphire
got her name

My mother used to muse she was a slave to passion
she liked fornication
liked it a lot
it helped rebuke
disappointments on her timeline
the other women in our walk-up
called her Jezebel
but not to her face
because she'd cut their pretty little derrières
rearrange their bodies with her devil's tongue

not because I was pitch blue-black like the gemstone
not even because she wanted me hard & unyielding
she named me after Sapphire Stevens from *The Amos 'n' Andy show*
I was never going to take it lying down
Sapphire is not the name of a slave

You could be as sweet as Weezy on *The Jeffersons*
My mother used to say it didn't matter anyway
if you was a strong black woman who stood her ground
they was going to find another name for you
like Esther
Florida
Florence
Maxine
Michelle

Stayed drunk

My father didn't mind being called out of his name
if he was drunk.

So, he stayed drunk.
His last name – *Hand* – suited him.

He had all 12 textbooks from Art Instruction, Inc,
published in the *Illustrator*, once.

His father told him he'd never amount to much,
he'd tell us kids, when he was drunk.

After the war, he thought he'd be a cartoonist
violinist, welder, or cook.

I don't remember what he did—
but mark my mother

with those hands.
Drunk! Drunk! Drunk!

DiVida archives 10 rules she learned in Kindergarten:

1. Wear flat shoes with rubber soles with plenty of room for your toes:
   easy to give chase
2. Eat all your vegetables: broccoli, spinach, kale, so you poop easily;
   sweet stuff is bad
3. Stay away from open windows, open fires, cut-out hearts
4. Disposables are good: friendships, relatives, societies, cultures, latitudes,
   geographies, planets, the universe, whatever doesn't serve you
5. Take turns in the kitchen area; don't get caught playing house with
   other little girls
6. If you want to kick someone, do it under the table
   (from the book of Sapphire)
7. Hugging is a no-no; keep your hands to yourself; don't touch your
   private parts
8. Stay in your seat; be quiet standing in line; no talking during lunch
   or at nap time
9. Learn to wipe your own butt and remember to wash your hands after
10. No meltdowns

DiVida becomes Captain of the Lacrosse Team

I have been kicked off the team.
DiVida is the only black girl allowed to play.
Her hair. It's natural, naturally like their hair combs,
mixed with lots of green jelly and mousse.

I am too sassy, sassiness is not allowed in Lacrosse.
I am kicked off for the team for the betterment of the team.
Gooey girls replace pawns, all the bishops, king and me.
They be pasty white, white like marshmallows.

It takes a lot of white to replace me. Sapphire runs
circles around the field, *I'm sorry Massa. Really I am.*
I won't talk back no more, she sings. *I promise*,
she says, with a wink, swinging the Lacrosse stick at me,

Why you wanna play with people who want to slave you?
The pasty marshmallows pull out a packet of Kools.
They smoke with long, heavy drags as DiVida goes up
in smoke extinguished. Lacrosse.

20

DiVida discovers she is fat, dumb and happy

at a picnic sponsored by the boss
He has brought his wife and children
They are dressed in suits and ties, even the little girl
Workers are dressed in polka-dot attire
They run around the park – happy
Everybody is happy – fucking happy
Children are swimming in the pool – happy
Overweight ones are happily playing on the seesaw
Wives are happy on the swings
Fathers are happy on the merry-go-round
The boss is standing under the gazebo – happy
Then it starts to rain — dangerous rain
Mean rain
Midnight horror movie in black and white rain
The workers — husbands, wives, single parents, children
Babies, teens, the handicapped, the fat, the dumb, the happy
Can't find shelter
The boss under the gazebo is speaking to the press
I said I would save money

Said I would bring down the cost of labor
Didn't I tell you we'd weather the storm

DiVida's hair starts to turn like Medusa
Sapphire on the sidelines — a dry crack in wet concrete
You'd never catch me at a picnic this time of year

DiVida travels First Class

I am standing in line at the train station.
Men in suits stand to the left and to the right of me
make other lines.

I am sitting at the head of the conference table.
Sapphire enters blowing a whistle: *All aboard broads*.
I want to interrupt the man who is talking.

I try to block the men who would push their way
past me in the line.
I am too big and tall to go unnoticed.

I wear a sandwich board sign: *Have opinions* is written
on one side
on the other side: *Need opinions? Get them here*.

Each time someone pushes past me in the line
the sign bellows: *Don't you see me standing here?*
The train becomes a graveyard.

In the conference room there is "going away" cake
balloons shaped like pens and pencils.
I ask who is retiring.

Someone says:
Some One who has her own opinions
who is trying to get on the train.

Sapphire is at the head of the table
wearing her birthday suit.
Her eyes tweak the "going away" speech:

This is a democracy. In a democracy, the majority decides who rides
in a democracy, it is decided. It is decided by the decided.
They decide who decides.

Everybody knows
if she wants to have opinions, she does not get to ride First Class.
We wish she who would have her own opinions a very good life.

The Highway Patrol stop DiVida

They want to see her
residency status

all she has is my passport
my picture

my place of birth
my expiration date

she tries to explain she is I
                    tells them

she is your try to do right
                walk right talk right she

walk the straight line obey
she

never get stopped by the police
she

when they look at her in disbelief she tells them
she is Skip Gates and this is her house I

wouldn't have been so nice and stagehand about it
I'd be, *What the Frankenstein?*

they'd wish they
had kept on going with their blinking lights

she wants to tell them
this ain't South Africa it's the USA   she doesn't want nobody

to (fill in the blanks)
she knows I don't have any time for backroads logic

I'm sorry, Officers, I say, *I forgot my ID*.

DiVida performs black face

Nina Simone is singing "Ain't Got No." She's
dressed in Afro-fashion, gold rings like fireflies.

The audience is already drunk when Dave Chappelle
enters. He tells a joke or two. They start to heckle.

Someone throws a shoe, then a banana at the stage.
Off beat, the crowd dances the chimpanzee shuffle.

DiVida comes on stage tap-dancing & rapping.
Part MC Hammer, part Howard "Sandman" Sims,

she huffs & puffs. Her black face drips insistent
becomes a puddle on the floor causing trips & slips.

The crowd gets louder and louder, jeers & cheers.
You would think they were at a barbeque or picnic.

What's that they're saying? *Lynch 'em. Lynch 'em.*
I swear some lines are just one syllable over da rules.

DiVida meets Trayvon Martin on the street and it is raining

He does not have an umbrella and does not speak. She thinks: What is a black boy doing out all alone especially in this neighborhood where it is not safe for black boys to be out alone or even in groups with or without an umbrella? What is he wearing? Even with that hood he is likely to get cold or run into someone who will leave him on the street wet.

DiVida tries to save the world

The President has sent the Secretary of State to the Middle East to negotiate peace. DiVida goes along to carry her briefcase and her pointer so when the Secretary has to give her PowerPoint presentation, she has a free hand to hold her skirt down. Otherwise her pointer may slip and she may blot out Iraq, Iran, and Egypt along with Pakistan. DiVida is proud to carry the Secretary's briefcase and pointer. It is her contribution in the war against terrorism. The Secretary needs someone to help her brush her teeth and keep her kinks from going back. DiVida is good at keeping things in their place.

DiVida searches for freedom in a loaf of bread

I am in the grocery store looking for multigrain
find puffy and white

I have to go to the bathroom but it is too cold to get out of bed
If I get out of bed to go to the bathroom the dream will end before I find
    the bread

Sapphire tries to help DiVida: *Just get the white bread*
Toasted with butter and jam You won't know the difference

DiVida stands on Main Street inside an open market
I've been on this same street many times before in many other dreams

Always looking for multigrain
Groundhogs are crawling in and out of huge holes along the side of the
    road

Across the street there is a vendor selling freshly baked bread
It smells like home
Sapphire is standing on an auctioneer's block hawking:

Get your freshly baked bread here I got oatmeal barley wheat and rye

Look at these pecs they're made from eating just the right kind of bread
No Wonder Bread in this belly No sugar No puffy stuff

Look I've got every one of my teeth
Solid strong bones good for lifting and baling

in DiVida's pockets—bubble gum wrappers

DiVida posts black

builds patterns with Lego blocks: round, square, round, square, circles
    back black,
stands on top of the Empire State Building dressed as Wonder Woman
    black,
lassos black, stands down Liberty architecture with Chicken Little poop
    black,
wages war with hope black,

wears dresses purchased at Target black,
trumps Emily Post in retro white on black,
divines, dismisses, disappears in black,
refuses refugee status black,

Black.
        connects elements already connected.
        talks about what should not be said.
        does not need to show the birth certificate.
        is   space within space, parallel, where in nowhere, black.

every Tom, Dick and Harry.
Beulah and Christine.
just trying to get by.

Black.

DiVida lives within her means

Eats beans
Sleeps on the sofa
Homeschools her progeny
Stuffs cardboard in her shoes
Washes her underwear in the sink
Grows tomatoes and cucumbers on windowsills
Spends her pension on travel to and from alternative universes

The President interrupts her favorite TV show with talk:

We will invest in medical research.
We will invest in clean energy.
We will invest in job training.
We will invest in education.

The rich don't need another tax cut—not if it means seniors can't eat.

Sapphire mimics: million, billion, trillion—say it fast bet you choke on
    your own spit

I only got two dollars in my wallet
I can't afford the American dream

Pass the joint and put some ice in my Hennessy

DiVida sees red at the Duke Ellington Memorial, Harlem USA

Two, four, six red Skyline buses pigeon-loop Harlem's borders.
Eight, ten red Skyline buses sync in time, block Ellington's gate.
One, two, three black women cane across red Skyline bus lanes.
Three, six, nine nude Grecian muses hold Duke at Harlem's gate.

Skyline buses double-decker whine before Ellington's shrine.
Basketballs bounce, cars whirr, trees faint at Harlem's gate.
Tourists climb Skyline buses in quick flip-flop swing time.
Five, seven, ten strollers, clowns, gunshots on these red lines.

Seven Skyline buses stop for ceremony, crowd the politicians.
Kennedy Chicken shack, condos, heritage at Ellington's wake.
Red Skyline buses at Duke's m emorial measure stasis time.
DiVida gives beauty queen wave at Harlem's memorial gate

mirrors Harlem's black-patented bronze man's lonely gait.

DiVida and Brain Man hide out at the Park and Ride

she learns monkey business with the history teacher
in the backseat of a Chevrolet
casino dice hanging from the rearview

on the radio—*Color Me Badd* "I Wanna Sex You Up"

cyclone amusement park ride
as they pop quiz their bodies in hideous
aspiration toward another statistic

on the radio Herodotus

DiVida succumbs along the ridges of Brain Man

the brain is wider than the sky…
the brain is deeper than the sea
———Emily Dickinson

her canoe carved from the gum tree
DiVida travels down

the river along the walnut shell
of a man she hardly knows

exactly at the equinox
all along his reptilian place

loves him harder there
wanting in a homo sapiens

state of need
she plants dopamine flowers

from river source to river mouth she travels
consumed

DiVida eats her cock and has it too

Baked red rooster and fried chicken wings splayed
on the repast table with potato salad fermenting
cheap perfume found in convenience
stores DiVida's hazy head. Ever since
her mother died she don't like meat that gets stuck
in her teeth or any kind of procreating
she's done with cock-a-doodle-doo or her will
make like a spider get full on
full mouth sacrifices swallowed whole
in loving memory of her mother.

DiVida reads Brain Man's tarot at the Shady Oaks Trailer Park in Mosquito City

Wide-legged in slippery heat and Fossil shoes
DiVida deals Brain Man five cards
Emperor, *Knight of Wands*, *King of Coins*, *The Hermit*
(one card hidden)

Brain Man can't figure things out is she charlatan or just weird
DiVida feigns her best psychic network speak
Reads from a teleprompter Sapphire holds:

Four-card stud you is like two games in one
Life is not beautiful all the time
We exist inside fenced-in dog run

So bark—arf, arf, arf, arf
Enjoy the bingo take a dip in the pool
Overeat at the potluck supper

Rule your doghouse four-card stud
or get what you give in equal portions like lunch in a pre-school

scoop of greens, ½ chicken sandwich, pickle slice, cup of milk
The locals don't want any trouble but the Sheriff got a limp and a
crooked eye
so go ahead shake your body Hazmat Modine is playing Hokum Jug
Band

Hoot like you unleashed Brain Man let your pants fall down
Take your Black stallion to the open road
Let fish gallop on your chest

Wave your wand in the air like you just don't care
Don't get stuck in a 52-card deck
or fry your main parts at both ends

Walk the daylight with a lamp
Wormhole your way through the universe
Squid ink anything that gets in your way

Sapphire deals herself six cards
face up the *High Priestess* four of a kind -
"Arròs Negre"

I am, you Brain Man are my slave
We'll meet again when you travel
Parliament Funkadelic – the one and only Pharoah

DiVida greets her Love Child at Walmart

DiVida tells Brain Man if he wants a Love Child he will have to give
birth to it she's not carrying no child not in her knapsack there are places
inside her head not suitable for a Love Child

He will have to figure out how to feed and cloth it too she's not swaddling
diapering or warming bottles her breasts are no longer suitable for a Love
Child

Maybe an account at Walmart will help they're nice there with nice
greeters that will float out to meet him with nice smiles she has too much
ill will in her smile which is definitely not suitable for a Love Child

It's like that sometimes I mean ridiculous life can be sometimes ridiculous
to DiVida, Brain Man looks too like Kanye sounds just like Kanye too
vision like this she knows is not suitable for a Love Child

A whole Saturn cycle later she's at Walmart this time with Sapphire
    waiting in the car
She and Brain Man's Love Child is at the door: *Hello, Welcome to Walmart*
    it grins

DiVida doesn't care who knows she's happy to see her Love Child
pretends she doesn't hear Sapphire scream from the car: *Don't forget to
return that American Dream and pick up some rainbow for the parade*

DiVida dresses like a man

cotton slacks shirts with stripes
lavender ties popular in spring
hip chains for keys padded thigh seams

she stands in the women's
line prefers the smell of a woman's
almond shaped unwashed sex a woman's

water; but today she gets ejected
for looking like a man; ejected
for absent-mindedly grabbing her crotch; ejected

for acting like a man
even when Sapphire hisses: *She ain't no man*
she just likes to dress like man

they demand that DiVida leave
who screams: *You can't ask me to leave*
cause I'm not feminine I won't leave
if you please

44

I will use the ladies room please
this is my gender identification please

even if I look like a man

DiVida guns the snow-white light

forces her brain to move in the opposite direction. She tries to make
the dancer turn counterclockwise. It doesn't matter what she eats for
breakfast, she can't get the bacon off the toast. Sometimes on her way
to work she sees things: bubble gum bazookas, pig's feet, random fairy
tales. At the office, the same thing: a red phone, a red lollipop, a red dildo.
When it all gets to be too much, she closes the door and masturbates on
the floor. In her favorite fantasy, she is naked inside a snow globe doing
her self with a crystal. She strokes and strokes herself while watching
Sapphire dance. Then she comes in a twist and a shout like a blizzard of
glass.

DiVida learns how to breathe

She cannot catch her breath. She tries to hold it when walking, talking and making love. But it keeps running away. She decides she must be dead. Her first memory of corpse-ness, she was nine. That was the year the sky stung like a bumblebee and the wet ground hollered. It hollered like a wet baby. It hollered like a wet baby with a chafed bottom, a bottom raw from having been left in a wet diaper too long.

She is in her room holding her breath so no one knows she is touching herself. Outside her room she hears her mother rain. She hears her father too. His hands booming. His voice crackling.

She does not really remember this. She read it in a book. A book marked *Vanity*.

Sapphire has positive and negative jumper cables clipped to her nipples. They cross her from left to right.

Sapphire coos: *Hold on baby. Let me put some towels under you. You're going to have multiple orgasms this time and I don't want your seism flooding the sheets.*

DiVida does a triolet

when she woke up early her stuff
gone her trowel her seed split
milking cow chicken free snuff
nothing to last her past winter
no horses no barn no handcuff
she was alone to contemplate
Sapphire had taken a furlough
gone even took her lush mittens

DiVida does herself

covered in polyurethane from head to toe a wrapper that fits so tight she
    can't feel
she's grown allergic to latex so sex is without question no longer possible
except for the maintenance woman who sweeps around the scene
of DiVida who wonders where she left her feet and slippers
so she decides to use Saran Wrap next time.

Sapphire on the intercom:

Today on sale
cheap final

DiVida reflects on what she knows about love

she remembers her first love
the lover that now seeks piety

covers her lust with Sunday-
go-to-meeting hats

worn for fear the Devil
asks for her body in a pine box

on her flat-screen queers sashay
red white & blue

whirls in her head a thicket
sound uncorked & bald

like a cheap refrigerator's whine
on the transistor archival

announcement of men landing
moon like exploration

sex on park benches with strangers
meet on the internet in layers

bundled lace hovering mid-air
the Apollo above a cut-out moon

first garbled noise: *one small step*
who cares about progress

first love doesn't sing
of romantic love, just God

Pussy Willow bop

DiVida's pussy willow is shaved clean
wiped with antiseptic that turns her skin green
for the doctor with the middle name Klauss
who slides a long tube from her groin to her heart
but instead finds a clock ticktock
doobe do dat fat cat

you can't make your heart feel something it won't

two poets in conversation
say the terrible makes the good possible
heebie-jeebies in the dark
doobe do dat fat cat

you can't make your heart feel something it won't

the male nurse
kisses her hand calls her dear
I told you dear I told you dear
in the dark
it's just a picture
doobe do dat fat cat

DiVida stays awake until day breaks (remixed)

 a round table in front of the window at the northern side of
the bed in prayer

her folded hands clasped against rain
icy drip from the IV

she wakes nods wakes
snaps back like from a broken hinge

is this what the hen feels in slaughter
timbre of cello strings breaking

rainwater de-crystallizing
like a defrosting freezer

rain against the air
slurping arrhythmia

welcomed touch of the technician's body against her falling
against sleep

DiVida contemplates the hard problem

at the banquet
rows and rows of hot buttered rolls
plates of steamed broccoli

crispy tofu with sesame
Sapphire outside chain-smoking with the men
girlfriends and boyfriends inside

DiVida at a table alone blue food serenades
lemon meringue cracks her graham
strawberry shortcake publicly displays her thighs

for the second day in the week
she hasn't been able to get out of bed
left toe right hip space bar thumb hurt

a repairman is at the door
Did you order a neural network biochemical engineer?
the hollow chocolate bunny answers: *You love yourself more than you love*
me

she bites into the bunny's thin skin
what doesn't break
stains her fingers

As yellow and sun shiny as a flip-top box of Rescue chewing gum

Orange & elderflower NDC# 057687-290-17.
The liquid center of a chewing gum sold at the health food store.
Rescue in bold yellow printed along the left side of the box homeopathic.
Active ingredients lost. Purpose: courage and presence of mind; focus when

ungrounded; patience with problems and people; softens the impact of
   shock
or the slipping grip when thrown off a building like the television star
who hangs on by one hand just long enough to be rescued for the grand
   finale.
A few drops under the tongue corrects emotional imbalances; also in a
   balm.

Keep out of reach of children. Don't use if pregnant or breastfeeding.
Like a pack of cigarettes but in a yellow box — may be addictive.
Excessive consumption may induce mild laxative effect. Not suitable
for animals. Are we something other than animal?

DiVida appropriates aftershock

after having survived 936 earthquakes in 28 days
she rides the subway home in sweaty pants

apologizes for disturbing good people
begs for spare change

little something to eat
break-dances the door

drums the aisles
with the bends

chalks her feet
with dust

Divida submits to her Duende

after throwing up mornings for months
after memorizing the entire Hallmark section
after all the walls in the kitchen have been painted yellow
after she has manicured the floors

colored her hair
put on her boxing gloves
she let loose the boogeyman
unchained the monkey on her back

Sapphire sucker-punches her in the gut
just to be sure
there is blood
there are tears

DiVida scoops her heart out

 like watermelon at a picnic or ice cream at the fair
sticky stuff dripping down her hands
traveling past her wrists to the crook of her arm.

She scoops without shame like a wife
at a funeral who loved unconditionally long
like an orgasm after a really good fuck.

She scans our faces.
Do we notice her public exposure
consider it indecent?

The Old People of Lambertville

will probably live forever with sunshine green trees and honey like the
old man crackling at the coffee counter straw hat and T-shirt revealing
his homogenized body is good and strong what does he need he must be
at least 90 still alive not dead like her mother at 81 told by the oncologist
she had lived long enough so if she stopped breathing no point in sticking
a tube down her throat because it would be painful more painful than she
could imagine and definitely not worth living for.

DiVida falls out of the sky

Sapphire is whispering in her ear
Force your body to the left we have to reverse the turn if we are going to live
DiVida is trapped in a car that is falling out of the sky
Sapphire's whisper is inside her head
Use your mind push your body around to the left against the turn of the sky
DiVida watches herself fall, piece by piece: hair, teeth, arms, legs
She is doing it she is breaking the fall leveling the sky's dark current
Turning into water

Rumor has it DiVida's taken a trip around the world and woke up right back where she started from

DiVida traveling by paddleboat on the icy blue Aegean Sea is whipped back and forth like a Ping-Pong ball. The alpha bitch has decided she ain't gonna get no sleep not less she wants to be a chimney sweep. Mary Poppins feeding the baby from the kitchen sink and Rufus got the ouzo. They each be dripping wet swimming like Cyclopes island to island, rocky beach to rocky beach. The wino got her bottle tied together like a raft grinning and shining the shoes of the lady of the house. Slept on the sofa again last night, two bites away from diabetic coma a chest full of compliant bees not butterflies. The flies hover stray dogs beg for food, enterprising felines raid the garbage dumps everybody in a stupor love for the drink, the sea, caramelized onions and juice squeezed from the lemon directly from the tree in your backyard. DiVida wonders what it would feel like to sail the open sea like a pirate taking what she needs without shame or regret. Living out a cabin lined with silver and jewels looted from churches and rich men's suits. What would it feel like to live in a monastery cut from stone that never trembled when the wind rocked the shutters and slammed doors where birds chirped and chickens roost.

What would it feel like to leave home and really find home.

Trees sway bend low bow
kiss pebbled beach full-bodied
African wind speaks

White-face

…I hear women screaming in the night
—Ekere Tallie

…for others to see you, is a form of validation…
"I you see you, therefore you exist."
—Mickalene Thomas

Ekere, that's me in the mirror
Mickalene, that's me lying on your sofa
cuddled in nakedness

That's me at Carnival
Day of the Dead parade painted in white
face a contorted scream

That's me: Noh dancer
man as a woman
virgin on the Cross mistaken for Jesus

Don't send me to space

bury me on high ground
let me starve
teeth chattering
body feast for vultures

DiVida becomes pine

evergreen coniferous with needle-shaped leaves woody cones
her thick and sticky sap turpentine her scent voluminous, audible

her arms her legs her buttocks her head her toes something to sit upon
soft like a cushion hard like a frame

the wood of any pine is widely used
for shade for timber for tar—inside its grove is languid longing

DiVida is all these things awkward and magnificent

get a grip Sapphire opines:
you is just like the rest of us beasts – you eat, you shit and you pray

the Almighty won't smite you, accidentally, while he is tending his
multitude
I got the secret for not getting lost in the fray – take the free

packets of needles 'n thread from motel bathrooms and the bars of soap
   too

let they who throw first stones at you be afraid

your plume's been here ever since the planet was covered in forest
and you really were a tree

a tree surrounded by water

Square root

…the useless prism of my own desires

—Jay Wright

how simple
it would be
if I were just a twin

but this life
carnival mirror

every flip & fall
a trapeze whirl

one minute you're standing erect
next you're kissing
the ground

DiVida dies

There is an accident on a slippery road
The doctors say: *Sorry no empty beds*

Huge lumps inside her solar plexus
pulse like they have their own hearts

The doctors are takeout food deliverymen
who say: *Sorry no credit just cash*

Sapphire sits in the audience
of a cable TV cooking show

The celebrity chef makes rice with kidney beans and liver
He says: *Remove the pulsing lumps from inside the body*

We don't need the body
Just toss the body once you have removed the heart

The audience flaps their arms like bodies on a slippery road
like bodies that think if they flap their arms they will find their balance

There is an awful beeping sound
Then no sound like a flat line

The nurse practitioner tells me all my tests are normal
I didn't die

That's not my body floating on the ceiling
That's Sapphire holding an umbrella

The Big House

I sit on a parcel of land
circling the Big House

where columns guard
like teeth

as if to grab your arms
& legs like a rabid dog's

a porch where lovers swing
watch stars as if by swinging

from a tree, feet suspended
like a pendulum

will swell their breathing
a big white house

with columns and a porch
room for a swing, as

I, she, he, they, we
sit on a parcel of land

ever present
on hallowed ground

one dark black
glove of mourning

the house laughs
the circle laughs back

we, the people watch
as the roof blackens

from our many
burning

Postman

I am a postman.
I saddle my horse in the middle of the night,
ride with bundles of mail through the forest like a shooting star.
They are afraid of me.
When I ride,
I am not a slave.

The forest flames
with talk of the blacks in Saint-Domingue.

They think, if they take my horse,
the earth will abandon me,
and I will no longer hear

trees.

The Happiest Day of My Life

the day I understood
hieroglyphics

knew the journey
home (almost there)

me in a loose-fitting skirt
that balloons

like a sail

I am no longer a cliché
not the only black girl on the porch

not the only one singing
Wilson Pickett

not the only natty dreadlock
tapping her foot

I played for the band

no compass necessary

the voyage across continents
was not rough

we traveled in deep time
in both directions

we drank and farted
laughed at disease got lost

my breasts cuddled my belly
by moon and by sunlight

How I found my lost language

They got so much things to say
                    —Bob Marley

Of severed hearts again made one
                    —Frances Ellen Watkins Harper

All these voices in my skin
like needles and pins
say speak

say: *Monica speak*
move your feet

I be knowing
I don't be lost I be found

I walk before the way
water, heat, seed say, wind
speak

do
I do

Book Benefactors

Alice James Books wishes to thank the following individuals who generously contributed toward the publication of DiVida:

Ross Gay

Ellen Doré Watson

For more information about AJB's book benefactor program, contact us via phone or email, or visit alicejamesbooks.org to see a list of forthcoming titles.

Recent Titles from Alice James Books

Alice James Books has been publishing poetry since 1973. The press was founded in Boston, Massachusetts as a cooperative wherein authors performed the day-to-day undertakings of the press. This collaborative element remains viable even today, as authors who publish with the press are also invited to become members of the editorial board and participate in editorial decisions at the press. The editorial board selects manuscripts for publication via the press's annual, national competition, the Alice James Award. AJB remains committed to its founders' original mission to support women poets, while expanding upon the scope to include poets of all genders, backgrounds, and stages of their careers. In keeping with our efforts to foster equity and inclusivity in publishing and the literary arts, AJB seeks out poets whose writing possesses the range, depth, and ability to cultivate empathy in our world and to dynamically push against silence. The press was named for Alice James, sister to William and Henry, whose extraordinary gift for writing went unrecognized during her lifetime.

DESIGNED BY
PAMELA A. CONSOLAZIO

Spark
design

Printed by McNaughton & Gunn